WordTOOLS For Athletes

Vol. 1

Harnessing the
Power of Words!

Carol L Rickard, LCSW

Well YOUniversity® Publications

Sign up now!

To be sure to get our weekly motivational & inspirational quotes and stories!

ThePowerOfWordsEQuote.com

Copyright © 2017 Carol L. Rickard

All Licensing by Well YOUniversity, LLC

All rights reserved.

ISBN-13: 978-1-947745-08-7

WordTools for Athletes Vol. 1

Harnessing the Power of Words!

by Carol L Rickard, LCSW

© Copyright 2017 Well YOUniversity Publications

ISBN 13: 978-1-947745-08-7

All rights reserved.

No part of this book may be reproduced for resale, redistribution, or any other purposes (including but not limited to eBooks, pamphlets, articles, video or audiotapes, & handouts or slides for lectures or workshops).

Licenses to reproduce these materials for those and any other purposes must be obtained from the author and Well YOUniversity.

888 LIFE TOOLS (543-3866)

Carol@WellYOUniversity.com

Welcome!

My 1st WordTool came to me in 2006 when doing a group with my patients. How could I get them to welcome change in their lives?

Creating **H**ealthy **A**nd **N**ew **G**rowth **E**xperiences!

From there it's been an onward journey! Most of them are inspired by persons or situations. My hope is to create Ah-Ah moments that can help change a life!

They are officially called "Artinyms", which is Sanskrit for "describe".

On the back of each wordtool is a question for you. Answering them will serve to strengthen your mind and your game!

~To Living Well TODAY! ~

Carol

WordTOOL Guide:

ACTION	1	EGO	31
ATTITUDE	3	EVALUATE	33
AWARE	5	EXCUSE	35
BLAME	7	FAILURE	37
CAN'T	9	FINISH	39
CHAOS	11	FOCUS	41
COMMIT	13	GOALS	43
CONSISTENT	15	HABIT	45
DETERMINED	17	IMPACT	47
DISCIPLINE	19	MIND	49
DO	21	MISTAKE	51
DON'T	23	PRACTICE	53
DOUBT	25	REACT	55
DREAM	27	START	57
EFFORT	29	TEAM	59

Sign up now!

To be sure to get our weekly motivational & inspirational quotes and stories!

ThePowerOfWordsEQuote.com

A
Critical
Task
Implemented
Only
Now!

COPYRIGHT 2017 & Licensed by Well YOUniversity, LLC

What **actions** do you need to take in order to raise your game to the next level?
What does not taking action cost you?

Adjust
Thinking
To
Intentionally
Take
Us
Direction
Excellence

COPYRIGHT 2017 & Licensed by Well YOUniversity, LLC

How would you describe your *attitude*?

Do you need to make some adjustments?

If so, what? If no, why not?

Actively

Work

At

Recognizing

Existence

COPYRIGHT 2017 & Licensed by Well YOUniversity, LLC

What have you been told by a coach/mentor that you need to become more *aware* of?

How will it impact your game if you do? If you don't?

Become

Lost

Amongst

Many

Excuses

COPYRIGHT 2017 & Licensed by Well YOUniversity, LLC

When was the last time you *blamed* someone or something instead of owning responsibility? How has blaming hindered your game?

Counts
As
Not
'
Trying

COPYRIGHT 2017 & Licensed by Well YOUniversity, LLC

What are some things you've told yourself you **can't** do? What have others said you can't do? How will your game improve if you were to just try?

Constantly

Having

Activity

Obstruct

Success

COPYRIGHT 2017 & Licensed by Well YOUniversity, LLC

What is the *chaos* you need to remove from your life in order to become a better athlete? How has chaos stopped you from having success in the past?

Challenge

Ourselves

Make

Matters

Important

Today!

COPYRIGHT 2017 & Licensed by Well YOUniversity, LLC

What is one thing that if you were to **commit** to it would make a huge positive difference in your game? What has stopped you?

Concentrate

On

Not

Stopping

Instead

Strengthen

The

Effort

Needed

Today!

COPYRIGHT 2017 & Licensed by Well YOUniversity, LLC

Make a list of all the things you need to become more *consistent* with that will raise your game to the next level:

Don't

Ever

Talk

Excuses

Recognizing

My

Intention

Needs

Exact

Direction!

COPYRIGHT 2017 & Licensed by Well YOUniversity, LLC

How are you **determined** to improve as an athlete in the next year? Where is it that you want your game to take you?

Deciding

I

Stay

Committed

In

Purpose

Letting

In

No

Excuses!

COPYRIGHT 2017 & Licensed by Well YOUniversity, LLC

How would you be better if you had more *discipline*? What's stopping you?

Direct
Opportunity

© 2017 & Licensed by Well YOUniversity, LLC

What is it you need to *do* to become a better athlete? A better person? A better scholar?

Denied

Opportunity

Not

'

Trying!

COPYRIGHT 2017 & Licensed by Well YOUniversity, LLC

What is it that you *don't* like to do?

How have you stopped yourself from achieving a higher degree of success as an athlete??

Dwell

On

Unfounded

Beliefs &

Thoughts

COPYRIGHT 2017 & Licensed by Well YOUniversity, LLC

What are some of the **doubts** you have about yourself? How would your game be different if they weren't there?!

Daringly

Recognize

Experiences

As

Mine

COPYRIGHT 2017 & Licensed by Well YOUniversity, LLC

What are some of your *dreams*?

Engage

Full

Force

On

Reaching

Target

COPYRIGHT 2017 & Licensed by Well YOUniversity, LLC

On a scale from 1 (low) to 10 (high), where would you put the level of **effort** you make in everyday practice? How can you improve it?

Establishes

Great

Obstacles

COPYRIGHT 2017 & Licensed by Well YOUniversity, LLC

Has your *ego* ever gotten too big?

If not, how do you keep yourself humble?

Extremely

Valuable

Activity

Letting

Us

Assess

True

Effectiveness

COPYRIGHT 2017 & Licensed by Well YOUniversity, LLC

What do you *evaluate* to be your strengths? What are some of your limitations you need to work on?

Engage

Xternal

Circumstances

Undermining

Self

Empowerment

COPYRIGHT 2017 & Licensed by Well YOUniversity, LLC

What have been some of the **excuses** you've made in the past regarding a poor performance? What was the real reason you did so poorly?

Find
An
Important
Lesson
Using
Real
Experiences

COPYRIGHT 2017 & Licensed by Well YOUniversity, LLC

What have been some of the *failures* you have had in your athletic career that have taught you the MOST? How about in life?

Focus

In

Now

Instead

Stopping

Halfway

COPYRIGHT 2017 & Licensed by Well YOUniversity, LLC

Make a list of all the things you have not **finished**.
Do each one & cross it off the list once done!

Fix

Our

Concentration

Until

Successful

COPYRIGHT 2017 & Licensed by Well YOUniversity, LLC

What are some areas of your game, which if you were to *focus* on, could take you to the next level?

Get

Our

Activity

Lined-up

Straight

COPYRIGHT 2017 & Licensed by Well YOUniversity, LLC

What are some of the *goals* you have for yourself in the next 6 months? Year?
What are some of your long term goals?

Having

A

Behavior

Internally

Triggered

COPYRIGHT 2017 & Licensed by Well YOUniversity, LLC

What *habits* do you need to get rid of in order to up your game? What new habits do you need to establish?

I
Make
Powerful
Adjustments
Concerning
Today

COPYRIGHT 2017 & Licensed by Well YOUniversity, LLC

In what ways do you have an *impact* on your team, your school, on other athletes?

Magnificent

Instrument

Needing

Direction

COPYRIGHT 2017 & Licensed by Well YOUniversity, LLC

How do you harness the power of your *mind* to help you have your best athletic performance? Does your mind tend to help you or hurt you?

Making

Incremental

Steps

Towards

Achieving

Key

Efforts

COPYRIGHT 2017 & Licensed by Well YOUniversity, LLC

What are some of the *mistakes* you've made, either in practice or a real match, where you have learned the most?

Purposely

Repeat

Activities

Critical

To

Improving

Core

Elements

COPYRIGHT 2017 & Licensed by Well YOUniversity, LLC

What are some skills that if you were to *practice* more often could really change your playing level?

Release

Emotion

And

Create

Trouble

COPYRIGHT 2017 & Licensed by Well YOUniversity, LLC

When was a time in your life where you **reacted** & made the situation worse? Have you been thrown out of a game? If so, what was the impact?

Swiftly

Take

Action

Reaching

Targets

COPYRIGHT 2017 & Licensed by Well YOUniversity, LLC

What have been some of the actions or goals you have not ***started*** yet?

Together

Embrace

A

Mission

COPYRIGHT 2017 & Licensed by Well YOUniversity, LLC

What has been one of your most rewarding *team* experiences so far?

About the Author

Carol L Rickard, LCSW, TTS, of Hopewell, NJ is founder & CEO of WellYOUniversity, LLC, a global health education company dedicated *to empowering individuals with the tools and supports to achieve lifelong wellness & recovery.*

Also known as **America's Wellness Ambassador**, Carol is a dynamic & engaging speaker who brings to life practical / useful solutions. She is a weekly contributor for Esperanza Magazine; written 13 books on stress and wellness, had a guest appearance on Dr. Oz last year

She is also the creator & host of a 30-minute wellness show on Princeton TV - **The WELL YOU Show** which current episodes are aired on Mondays at 6:00pm EST & Sundays at 8:30am EST and can be watched at PrincetonTV.org.

All episodes available at: **www.TheWELLYOUShow.com**

Get more of Carol at:

Twitter: ***@wellYOUlife***

"Like us" @ www.FaceBook.com/WellYOUniversity

Have Carol Speak at Your Next Event!

Get more information about how you can have Carol speak at your organization, event, or conference.

Go to: www.CarolLRickard.com

Or call: 888 Life Tools (543-3866)

Carol's Other Books

Getting Your Mind to Mind You
ANGER – A Simple & Practical Approach
Help – How to Help Those Who DON'T Want it
Selfness – Simple Self-Care Secrets
Stress Eating – How to STOP Using Food to Cope
Stretched Not Broken – Caregiver's Stress
The Caregiver's Toolbox
Transforming Illness to Wellness
Putting Your Weight Loss on Auto
The Benefits of Smoking
Moving Beyond Depression
LifeTools – How to Manage Life
Creating Compliance
Relapse Prevention

Please visit us at:

www.WellYOUniversity.com

Sign up for weekly motivational e-quote!

Check out our upcoming FREE webinars!

Learn more about our training programs.

Email us your success story at:

Success@WellYOUniversity.com

We'd like to ask for your feedback

Please check out the next page
if this book has been HELPFUL for you!

We'd love to hear from you!

Feedback Card

Please take a moment & provide us some feedback about the book you just read & how you feel *it benefited YOU!*

_____

_____

_____

_____

Name: _____

Best Phone #: _____

Can we use your comments in our publicity materials?
Yes / No

If OK with you, what's the best time to call you:_____

Thank You!

Scan or take a picture & email:
Carol@WellYOUniversity.com

Snail mail: Carol Rickard
5 Zion Rd., Hopewell, NJ 08535

Tear along here

www.ingramcontent.com/pod-product-compliance
Lightning Source LLC
LaVergne TN
LVHW051850080426
835512LV00018B/3174